# WOMAN of *worth*

## LIFELONG EMPOWERMENT FROM PSALM 139

# RUTH COGHILL

WOMAN OF WORTH

Copyright © 2011 by Ruth Coghill

WORDS to *Inspire*
Lifelong Empowerment From God's Word

Library and Archives Canada Cataloguing in Publication

Woman of worth / Ruth Coghill.

ISBN 978-0-9865980-9-8

1. Coghill, Ruth. 2. Christian women--Religious life. 3. Self-esteem in women--Religious aspects--Christianity. 4. Bible--Criticism, interpretation, etc. I. Title.

BV4527.C64 2011 248.8'43 C2011-902692-9

WHAT OTHERS HAVE SAID ABOUT

## *Woman of Worth*

"*Woman of Worth* speaks straight to the heart. Full of transparency and rooted deeply in the Word of God, Ruth offers wisdom gleaned from experiences and from knowledge discovered in God's Word and applied to her heart. The applications of each lesson clearly mark the paths to overcoming the emotional and spiritual challenges each one of us faces in our daily journey. This study will transform your life."

Eileen Stewart-Rhude, Author
*The Leadership Edge—Seven Keys to*
*Dynamic Christian Leadership for Women*

"Ruth Coghill speaks and writes with a sweet vulnerability and quiet power, explaining from her own long experience how the deep truths from God's Word can become both alive and life to those who love him. That openness builds vital bridges: between herself and her audience, and her audience and our Lord Jesus Christ—the only bridge to God."

Kathleen Gibson, Speaker, Author
*Practice by Practice—The Art of Everyday Faith*

"A great Bible study has two elements: a truth drawn directly from Scripture, and a personal experience to illuminate that truth and focus it like a laser beam deeply into the human heart. Ruth Coghill's studies have both elements."

Ray Wiseman
Winner 2009 Leslie K. Tarr Award

# Dedication

*To Mom and Dad (Clara and Bernard Tatton)*
*whose devotion, commitment and love for God*
*and His Word instilled in me a desire for the same.*
*Although our family vessel pitched and rolled on*
*the angry waves of life, my rich heritage provided*
*an anchor that kept me from drifting too far*
*away. I am forever grateful.*

# TABLE OF CONTENTS

# A NOTE FROM RUTH

I am so thankful that you have picked up this newly expanded *Woman of Worth* four-lesson guide. Set up for either group or personal study, the practical applications packed into this Bible study are both powerful and simple, a great study for women longing to understand a sense of their value in God's eyes.

If you choose to lead a group, you might find there is more material in one lesson than you can cover, depending on the allotted time slot. Because of that, the study is purposely called four *lessons* instead of four *weeks*. As a facilitator, ask God to give you creative ways to make *truth* come alive to each participant. Watch for opportunities to use visuals, as in lesson three, a stamp pad. Not one of us can change another, but as we journey together, pursuing a relationship with our creator, God will mould hearts and shape desires.

I learned long ago that the most important reason to study the Bible is not for *information* alone, but for *transformation*. An inexplicable change occurs when we take time to excavate nuggets of truth and makes any effort well worthwhile, enabling us to embrace God's purpose and plan for our lives.

Reaching deep within, I've chosen personal, emotionally-packed, life-altering experiences to begin every lesson. What a privilege to share with you. Perhaps as you go through these truths from Psalm 139, you too can begin a personal journal to record the reality of God's transforming power.

Well, if you are ready, let's get started!

Enjoying the Son,

*Ruth*

## *Lesson One*
## GOD KNOWS ME

I was a failure and I knew it. Feelings of guilt, fear and inadequacy enveloped my whole being, hiding the brilliant-blue northern sky from my view. Nothing made any sense. I had a husband and family who loved me, as well as a great teaching position. It wasn't enough.

Disappointment with my personal performance, immediately followed by discouragement, sent me spinning into a downward spiral toward a pit of depression. My self-worth plummeted to an all-time low, leaving me with the thought, *I'll never teach again.*

It all started with a special board assignment in northern Ontario during the early days of the open-concept environment. With just three years of teaching experience, I felt honoured to host one of the experimental classrooms. I loved each primary child who entered my doors, and spent hours trying to prove my worth and competency. I made sure my room displayed the best bulletin boards, the finest visual aids and the quietest group of six-year-olds to walk the hallways for recess or assembly. I arrived at school when the doors opened and stayed long after most other staff had left. My goal—to be the best teacher in the area.

The following spring, the inspector came for his evaluation. His primary purpose was to analyze the new system and compare its results to the more traditional methods of teaching, as well as to provide my annual report. I relished the opportunity to show off my skills with my pupils and expected a top-notch rating. However, he did not appreciate the changes that brought such freedom to the children.

At first, I listened. But soon I considered each negative comment and suggestion to be personal disapproval. My heart sank as I internalized every word. For the first time in my teaching career, my report was not stellar.

The next day, it took great effort to enter the classroom. I could not wait for the school day to end. When it did, I could not wait to go to bed. Once comfortably tucked in for the night, sleep eluded me. I tossed and turned, replaying every word uttered by the board's official. I thought I could sleep this horrible feeling off, except I could not settle down into slumber.

*Perhaps I can laugh it off, cry it off.*

That did not work. I longed to awaken to a new day, experiencing the joy I had prior to "the visit."

After several sleepless nights, I drove to the drug store. "I need something to help me sleep," I said to the pharmacist. He gave me an over-the-counter medication but advised me to go to my family doctor.

I dreaded a trip to my physician, for by now I felt nauseous every morning while preparing for the school day. Headaches became my uninvited but frequent guests. I struggled more every minute. Soon despair walked on in.

The doctor suggested a break from teaching, but with summer approaching, I confidently assured him the two months off would repair all damage and I would be ready as usual for September. I planned my strategy. *I'll not try so hard. I'll just be casual, not such a perfectionist.*

September arrived. It wasn't long before I realized my vacation plan lacked any positive results. My heart raced while preparing lessons. Entering the classroom felt like approaching the foot of a rugged mountain, with the thirty-five children sitting, waiting at the insurmountable peak. Ill-equipped to make the climb, I panicked. A week off to spend time at a psychiatric clinic in Toronto only brought more feelings of hopelessness. Bob and I drove in silence back to North Bay. Defeated again, I sank deeper into despondency.

"Ruth you need to resign from teaching for now. You cannot carry on like this," my doctor said. He wrote out his orders to the board for my dismissal and across the top, in big letters, he added the words, "poor mental health."

Those words read like a death sentence, their message screaming "Loser". With my family's history of mental illness, I had tried all my life to avoid any such sickness.

I dragged one foot in front of the other as I left the doctor's office, my *best teacher* dream ripped to shreds. Anti-depressants now part of my daily intake, I had to face the fact that I was smack in the middle of a major depression. Once freed of the responsibility of the classroom, the absence of any productivity or accomplishment in my days emphasized my failure. Months slowly passed by, each attempt to crawl out of the slimy pit meeting with another slippery slide further down. Darkness presented fear and daylight brought yearning for night. "Oh God, please get me out of this horror" was my continuous plea.

1. Have you ever felt such worthlessness?
   List words to describe your feelings.

   _____

   _____

   _____

2. What were the circumstances
   surrounding the above?

   _____

   _____

   _____

   _____

If you have experienced such desperation, you are not alone. David, Israel's greatest king, also suffered from despair. At times his depression arose out of the circumstances surrounding him, and at other times from his own personal weaknesses, his failures. As the youngest of Jesse's sons, a shepherd, even his father doubted his potential when Samuel came to anoint the next king. David's mastery of the harp pleased King Saul until David won favour in the eyes of the people. Saul's jealousy began a season of running for David. Throughout the Psalms, David questioned his thoughts, his worth and God's care for him. Listen as he describes his experience in this Psalm 13 prayer:

[1] How long, O Lord?
   Will you forget me forever?
   How long will you hide your face from me?

[2] How long must I wrestle with my thoughts
    and every day have sorrow in my heart?
    How long will my enemy triumph over me?

[3] Look on me and answer, O Lord my God.
    Give light to my eyes or I will sleep in death;

[4] My enemy will say, I have overcome him,
    and my foes will rejoice when I fall.

[5] But I trust in your unfailing love;
    my heart rejoices in your salvation.

[6] I will sing to the Lord,
    for he has been good to me.

                    *   *   *   *

3.  What thoughts did David express
    in verses 1-2?

    _____

    _____

    _____

4.  Had God forgotten David?
    If not, why did David feel this way?

    _____

    _____

    _____

In my mind, I wore a name tag on which was written the word FAILURE.

The time came when I knew I could not face another day like the ones of the previous months. Tired of my tears and hopelessness, and ashamed of my inadequacies, I fell on the floor, flat on my face, and prayed, "God, if you'll just get me out of this depression, I'll do anything you want me to do."

No flashing lights, no voice from heaven, just stillness.

My journey back to wholeness took many months but it began that day in our little apartment. I did not get up or move from that humble position until I had repented for attempting to live life my own way, and made the decision to put God's Word into my life. My parents had taught me that the Bible had the answers to all of life's problems. Now I had the responsibility to personally apply those truths.

I began to read and pray daily with new motivation, in spite of the negative thoughts that still lingered. I determined to believe what God said and committed myself to finding out what He meant. Read verse 5 of Psalm 13.

5.  What does David determine to do?

_____

_____

_____

_____

_____

You cannot see *trust* for it is an inner work, a resolution to believe wholly in something or someone. For too long I trusted in my own ability, my own efforts. David put his trust in God's unfailing love, the only place worthy of such an investment.

Grant Mullen, in his book, *Why Do I Feel So Down When My Faith Should Keep Me Up?*, wrote of his interest in pain control through general and local anaesthesia. "I was surprised to discover that more people were suffering from emotional pain than from physical pain,"[1] he said. He also uncovered the fact that to most people, "the most painful moment in their lives was from emotional, not physical pain." His book is a great resource for exploring this topic and includes the different causes of depression.

Many things can influence our sense of worth or lack thereof. Questioning, then doubting, my own worth sent me on a downhill slide. In book two of the WOW series, *Woman of the Word*, I will share three lies that held me captive, and the process I went through to replace those lies with truth. But for now, as we begin this *Woman of Worth* study, we will explore Psalm 139 in light of God's characteristics to glean a better understanding of Him, who He says we are and what our value is in His eyes. Embracing truths such as these will enable us to reach our godly potential.

Let's stand and read Psalm 139 together. Suggestion: have four different participants each read one of the six-verse sections.

---

1   Grant Mullen, *Why Do I Feel So Down When My Faith Should Lift Me Up?* (Kent, England: Sovereign World, 1999), 11.

## Psalm 139:1-6

*Characteristics of God:* _____

_____

¹ O LORD, you have searched me
     and you know me.

² You know when I sit and when I rise;
     you perceive my thoughts from afar.

³ You discern my going out and my lying down;
     you are familiar with all my ways.

⁴ Before a word is on my tongue
     you know it completely, O LORD.

⁵ You hem me in—behind and before;
     you have laid your hand upon me.

⁶ Such knowledge is too wonderful for me,
     too lofty for me to attain.

\*    \*    \*    \*

*Characteristics of God:* _____

_____

⁷ Where can I go from your Spirit?
   Where can I flee from your presence?

⁸ If I go up to the heavens, you are there;
   if I make my bed in the depths, you are there.

⁹ If I rise on the wings of the dawn,
   if I settle on the far side of the sea,

¹⁰ even there your hand will guide me,
   your right hand will hold me fast.

¹¹ If I say, "Surely the darkness will hide me
   and the light become night around me,"

¹² even the darkness will not be dark to you;
   the night will shine like the day,
   for darkness is as light to you.

\*   \*   \*   \*

*Characteristics of God:* _____

_____

¹³ For you created my inmost being;
    you knit me together in my mother's womb.

¹⁴ I praise you because I am
    fearfully and wonderfully made;
    your works are wonderful,
    I know that full well.

¹⁵ My frame was not hidden from you
    when I was made in the secret place.
    When I was woven together
    in the depths of the earth,

¹⁶ your eyes saw my unformed body.
    All the days ordained for me
    were written in your book
    before one of them came to be.

¹⁷ How precious to me are your thoughts, O God!
    How vast is the sum of them!

¹⁸ Were I to count them,
    they would outnumber the grains of sand.
    When I awake, I am still with you.

\* \* \* \*

*Characteristics of God:* _____

_____

¹⁹ If only you would slay the wicked, O God!
  Away from me, you bloodthirsty men!

²⁰ They speak of you with evil intent;
  your adversaries misuse your name.

²¹ Do I not hate those who hate you, O LORD,
  and abhor those who rise up against you?

²² I have nothing but hatred for them;
  I count them my enemies.

²³ Search me, O God, and know my heart;
  test me and know my anxious thoughts.

²⁴ See if there is any offensive way in me,
  and lead me in the way everlasting.

\*  \*  \*  \*

For this week we will focus on the first six verses.

6. What characteristics of God do you see in the first six verses? Record these below as well as on the lines provided on page 8.

_____

_____

_____

_____

7. From these verses make a list of the things God knows.

_____

_____

_____

_____

8. Who does God know according to verse 1?

_____

_____

_____

_____

*Searched*, according to Strong's concordance, comes from the root word, *to penetrate*, and means *to examine intimately*.[2]

I certainly did not want anyone to search my inner being, to know my thoughts those dreadful months. Each Sunday, I donned my hat, tucked a King James Bible under my arm and walked properly beside my husband, Bob, to find our pew. On occasion, we sang a duet during worship, blending in perfect harmony, offering no indication of the turmoil inside. No one could see the gut-wrenching pain, the agony of being a phony. I did not want anyone to know my embarrassing secret: I'm a depressed Christian, filled with guilt and insecurity, and on medication to help me face the day. I fooled a lot of people for some time, but not for a moment did I fool God. He knew. He searched. He examined intimately, not to harm but to heal.

9.  What do the following phrases from Psalm 139 mean or involve?

    a) "when I sit" and "when I rise" (verse 2)

    _____

    _____

    b) "my thoughts from afar" (verse 2)

    _____

    _____

---

2   James Strong, S.T.D., LL.D, *Strong's Exhaustive Concordance of the Bible* (Iowa Falls, IA: Riverside Book and Bible House), 43.

c) "my going out and my lying down" (verse 3)

_____

_____

_____

d) "familiar with all my ways" (verse 3)

_____

_____

_____

e) "Before a word is on my tongue
   you know it completely" (verse 4)

_____

_____

_____

f) "You hem me in" (verse 5)

_____

_____

_____

In reference to verse 6, *Believer's Bible Commentary* says, "His knowledge boggles the mind."[3]

(I have often wondered if God knows what I'm going to say, why doesn't He close my mouth before I open it and embarrass myself?)

10. What are some of your thoughts right now?

_____

_____

_____

The Bible gives us suggestions for proper thinking:

"Finally, brothers, whatever is true, whatever is noble, whatever is right, whatever is pure, whatever is lovely, whatever is admirable—if anything is excellent or praiseworthy—think about such things." (Philippians 4:8)

11. Underline each suggestion for good thinking in the verse above.

12. How much does God know about us?

_____

_____

_____

_____

---

3   William MacDonald, *Believer's Bible Commentary* (Nashville, TN: Thomas Nelson Publishers, Inc., 1989), 769.

Read this example that Jesus shows us regarding God's all-knowing process:

## JOHN 1:47–50

[47] When Jesus saw Nathanael approaching, he said of him, "Here is a true Israelite, in whom there is nothing false."

[48] "How do you know me?" Nathanael asked.

Jesus answered, "I saw you while you were still under the fig tree before Philip called you."

[49] Then Nathanael declared, "Rabbi, you are the Son of God; you are the King of Israel."

[50] Jesus said, "You believe because I told you I saw you under the fig tree. You shall see greater things than that."

13. What did Jesus answer when Nathanael asked, "How do you know me?"

_____

_____

_____

14. How did Nathanael respond?

_____

_____

_____

15. Who is the most important person you have
    known on earth? Do they know you?

_____

_____

_____

What a thought! The creator of the universe, the maker of heaven and earth, knows me, everything about me, more than I know about myself.

To fully embrace this truth is the first step to understanding our deep value. God knows my name, and He knows your name. WOW! You and I are not a number on a roster. We are personally known by the Master Designer. The Bible records long lists of names and generations. Each person, identified with a unique name, is significant in God's kingdom. Exodus 1:1 reads, "These are the names of the sons of Israel..." and every name follows.

Psalm 139:1-6 teaches that God knows everything. Now, there is something that God wants us to know.

## Jeremiah 9:23-24

> 23 "This is what the Lord says: 'Let not the wise man boast of his wisdom, or the strong man boast of his strength, or the rich man boast of his riches 24 but let him who boasts boast about this: that he understands and knows me, that I am the Lord, who exercises kindness, justice and righteousness on earth, for in these I delight, declares the Lord.'"

16. In what does the Lord want us to boast? What is it He wants us to know and understand?

_____

_____

_____

17. Note several of God's characteristics in these verses. List them here.

_____

_____

_____

# Hosea 4:6

"My people are destroyed from lack of knowledge.
Because you have rejected knowledge,
I also reject you as my priests;
because you have ignored the law of your God,
I also will ignore your children."

18. According to Hosea, how important is knowledge?

_____

_____

_____

19. Have you ever wondered why you feel so empty? In what ways have you tried to fill this emptiness?

_____

_____

_____

_____

_____

I have tried to fill that emptiness with my career, my mate, my children, my home and my hobbies. They have never been enough to fill the gap. That deep longing can only be filled by knowing and loving God. Ecclesiastes 3:11 says that eternity is planted in the hearts of all men. Since we have been created to live forever, nothing short of knowing the eternal God will satisfy us for the long haul.

The amazing fact is that God knows us intimately and is involved in our lives. He does not want us to know *about* Him, He wants us to know Him. To fully embrace this truth is life-altering. I can know God. I can only be changed as I come to know Him. There is a world of difference between knowing about God and knowing Him. I may believe that He is big, that He controls the weather and is involved in creation, but until I begin my intentional journey to know Him, what I believe about Him may or may not be correct. That's why I need a reliable source of truth about God, found in His Word, the Bible.

God is the one that initiates knowing us. Consider the following:

1 JOHN 3:1

> "How great is the love the Father has lavished on us,
> that we should be called children of God! And that is
> what we are! The reason the world does not know us is
> that it did not know him."

Book 2 in this *WOW* series, *Woman of the Word*, explores various practical ways of putting God's word into your life on a daily basis and, when applied, will enable you to learn more about Him. But for now, let's look at:

DANIEL 11:32 NASB

> "And by smooth words he will turn to godlessness those
> who act wickedly toward the covenant, but the people who
> know their God will display strength and take action."

20. What happens to those who know their God?
    Is this enough to make knowing God a prior-
    ity in your life?

 

_____

_____

_____

21. How can we know God?

_____

_____

_____

In his book, *Experiencing God,* Henry Blackaby writes, "You will never be satisfied just to know about God. Really knowing God only comes through experience as He reveals Himself to you."[4]

Now it gets more exciting!

22. What has God revealed to you about Himself
    in Psalm 139: 1-6?

_____

_____

_____

There is only one way to get to know someone and that is by spending time with him or her. I may have lots of information about a celebrity—the number of children she has, her spouse's name and any number of other statistics—but there is no relationship until there is a conversation, interaction and time invested. The more time spent with someone, the better we know him or her.

A number of years ago, I wanted to know God more intimately. I chose a place in our living room, an antique blue velour armchair. Each morning, before the children were up, I went to this spot for my appointment with God. I knew that developing a relationship of any kind required spending time with that person. I knelt down and began my prayer, *Lord I want to know you.* Within a very few minutes, sometimes even seconds, I was fast asleep. At first I felt such discouragement, as though I could never accomplish what I had set out to do. But then, I began to realize that I had taken a first step. God loved my getting up. Eventually, I began a prayer journal. I did not fall asleep while I wrote.

---

4   Henry T. Blackaby and Claude V. King, *Experiencing God* (Nashville, TN: Broadman & Holman Publishers, 1994), 5.

It's been over twenty years now, and I still consider that meeting at my old chair the beginning of a deeper adventure with God. I often failed at my appointments but never have I regretted those early risings.

## JOHN 17:3

"Jesus said: 'Now this is eternal life; that they may know you, the only true God, and Jesus Christ whom you have sent.'"

23. What do you know about God at this stage in your life?

_____

_____

_____

24. Where did you get the basis for your beliefs?

_____

_____

_____

25. Describe your desire to know God.

_____

_____

_____

Just because I believe something does not make it true. And just because I do not believe something does not mean that it is not true. How often I have not believed the truth about my loving Heavenly Father.

> 26. Are you willing to adjust your life in order to make time for your relationship with God to grow? In what ways?
>
> _____
>
> _____
>
> _____

It has been said that we change for one of two reasons: inspiration or desperation. Personally, my change began because of sheer desperation. The hole-in-the-soul feeling had taken up residence in my life long enough. False messages bombarded my mind. They needed to be replaced so that I could find my place to serve.

Replacing lies with truth enabled me to return to the classroom, evidence of the power of God's Word in my lifelong process of maintaining a healthy self-worth. Rehearsing the truths of God's Word will always increase understanding of our true value.

# God knows everything

## God knows me (_____)

Print your name on the line above

# Names and characteristics I am learning about God

You can add to this list each week.

1. _____

2. _____

3. _____

4. _____

5. _____

6. _____

7. _____

8. _____

9. _____

10. _____

11. _____

12. _____

## Points to Ponder:

"Inside each of us there is a God-shaped vacuum that can only be filled by God."

BLAISE PASCAL

"We tend by a secret law of the soul to move toward our mental image of God. What comes to mind when we think about God is the most important thing about us."

A.W. TOZER

"Failure is not a person. It is an event."

ZIG ZIGLAR

"Self-esteem can be affected by childhood experiences such as neglect and wounding words that, when heard repeatedly, can be internalized by a child. Laid down in childhood, these experiences form what we call our 'core beliefs,' what we think about ourselves and who we believe we are."

DR. LIBBY SKIDMORE

"Wisdom is meaningless until our own experience has given it meaning."

BERGEN EVANS

To hide in my heart:

"You hem me in—behind and before. You have laid your
hand upon me." (Psalm 139:5)

_____

_____

_____

_____

_____

_____

_____

_____

_____

_____

_____

_____

_____

_____

_____

_____

_____

_____

_____

_____

_____

_____

_____

_____

_____

_____

_____

_____

_____

_____

_____

_____

_____

_____

_____

_____

# *Lesson Two*

## GOD IS WITH ME

There are times when I have no earthly explanation for what I am experiencing. I can't see, hear or touch Him, but I am totally aware that the King of heaven has left His throne to descend to my terrain. Although I know God is everywhere and longs to be part of my day, when His presence is palpable, it never fails to take me by surprise.

Each Wednesday night last fall, a group of ladies studied Beth Moore's *Believing God*. At the end of the video one night, Beth encouraged all participants to tie a blue ribbon on their wrists to remind them of God's promises.[5] The idea springs out of Numbers 15:37-41, in the Old Testament, where the priests were instructed to wear tassels

5  Beth Moore, *Believing God* (Nashville, TN: Broadman & Holman Publishing Group, 2004). Session one of the video series.

with a blue cord around the bottom of their robes. This colourful trim attached to the edge of the garment helped bring to their minds all of God's commands, keeping them close at hand. I secretly questioned the value of the simple exercise, but wanted to join in with all the other girls. My choice was an elastic, royal-blue cord, one that was easy to remove when necessary.

While driving home, many thoughts swirled around in my head. Why do I need this cheap adornment? I believe God's Word. After all, I teach it regularly. From there, doubt crept in. *Are you sure you can write articles, let alone a book? It's been a long time since you started that project. Did God really say He wanted you to write?*

A prick of my conscience awakened me to the stark realization that, once again, I was listening to the wrong voice. *Lord, show me.*

*Ruth, do you really believe I am interested in your speaking and writing? Are you aware that it is not about you and your limitations, but about me and my plan?* By the time I arrived home there remained no question: I needed to believe more fully God's call on my life in specific areas of ministry. Humbled by my frequent doubts and self-centred inner thoughts, I asked the Lord to again confirm His call for me to write.

Very early the next morning, with the blue ribbon tied on my wrist, I left for the gym to take part in a *spin class.* Being new to this sport— pedalling furiously on the spot—I walked over to the same bike I had used previously, hoping a more familiar ride would help. Although no one occupied the seat as yet, a water bottle was nestled in the bike's holder. Disappointed and frustrated at the thought of adjusting another machine to my short arms and legs, I scanned the thirty different bicycles for another available one. Following the assistance of a helpful instructor, who made the necessary changes to accommodate my frame, I jumped on the new cycle. I began moving through the first stage, and then on to the climb, using gears to manoeuver each of the progressive inclines. Up the first mountain I pedalled slowly, warming up and then gaining speed. Although stationary, it took great effort to pedal that bike to the top. Panting, puffing and longing for the decline, I put my head down and prayed, *Lord you'll have to help me.* Exerting the last bit of energy I had, I lowered my eyes and gasped, scarcely believing what I was seeing. A royal-blue ribbon hung from the handlebar.

*Perhaps they've had some colour-coded team endeavour.*

Lifting my head, I looked for ribbons on the remaining bikes around the exercise room, thinking they all must have one. But no ribbon adorned any other bike, just mine. A fresh shot of adrenaline coursed through every fibre of my overheated body. With renewed motivation, I finished the hour, every second revelling in His presence. So personal. Just for me? Once again, I was reminded that God's promises are freely flowing and, yes, for me.

As I write today, the memory of that early morning still thrills me. What saddens me are all the times I have missed such adventure, such sheer pleasure, the fullness that Jesus promises in John 10:10: "I have come that they might have life and have it to the full."

I do not know how the blue ribbon managed to be tied on my bike that day, but I do know one reason—it was a personal reminder of the King's presence in my life.

That workout occasion deepened my desire to experience and enjoy my time with Him. I called it a majestic moment. Majestic, for the King of Kings in all His glory, in all His splendour, joined me in the gym for a few minutes. Well, in reality, He was there all the time, but He caused me to be aware.

In his book, *The Applause of Heaven*, Max Lucado states, "So grateful are we for his presence that we yearn for more of him (we hunger and thirst)."[6]

---

6  Max Lucado, *The Applause of Heaven* (Dallas, TX: Word Publishing, 1990), 10.

Max calls it sacred delight. "It is sacred because it is not of this earth... It is delight because delight can both satisfy and surprise."[7] Oh yes!

This week, we will explore the next six verses of Psalm 139, and then discuss ways that we can respond to His presence in our lives.

Let's stand and read Psalm 139: 7-12, found on page 9.

1. What characteristics of God do you see in these verses? Record these below as well as on the lines provided on page 9.

   _____

   _____

   _____

Did you know that verses 8 to 10 are carved in the marble panels on the south wall of the Memorial Chamber in the Peace Tower at the Parliament buildings in Ottawa?

2. According to verse 7, where can we go to get away from God's presence?

   _____

   _____

3. What two directions are indicated in verse 8? What two directions are indicated in verse 9? Describe the picture painted here. All spatial reality is covered in these verses.

---

7   Max Lucado, *The Applause of Heaven* (Dallas, TX: Word Publishing, 1990), 8.

_____

_____

_____

4. *Your right hand* is significant to God's character. Research and describe its meaning.

_____

_____

_____

5. Verses 10 to 12 give insight into what happens to darkness when God is present. On
   the lines below, describe a time in your life
   when you felt darkness all around. Find a
   verse from the text that tells where God was
   at this time. How does knowing that God
   is everywhere affect how you respond to the
   blackness of night?

_____

_____

_____

_____

I shared about my depression in Lesson One. During that time
in my life, I had a head knowledge that God's presence reigned, but I

had not yet experienced the reality of His omnipresence. I lived in the world of doing things for God. Striving. He wanted me to learn that He delights in simply being with me.

## ZEPHANIAH 3:17

> "The LORD your God is with you,
> he is mighty to save.
> He will take great delight in you,
> he will quiet you with his love,
> he will rejoice over you with singing."

There is no other friend who can be with you all the time, every minute, every hour, with or without make-up, dirty or clean, happy or sad. My prayer is that, before this week is over, you will become surprisingly aware that He is with you, longing for you to believe that truth.

In light of these six verses, any attempt to hide from God seems ludicrous. Nonetheless, many have tried. Perhaps, like me, you haven't consciously tried to hide from God, but simply left Him out of your life.

Let's learn from these examples:

## GENESIS 3:1-13

> [1] Now the serpent was more crafty than any of the wild animals the LORD God had made. He said to the woman, "Did God really say, 'You must not eat from any tree in the garden'?"

> [2] The woman said to the serpent, "We may eat fruit from the trees in the garden, [3] but God did say, 'You must not eat fruit from the tree that is in the middle of the garden, and you must not touch it, or you will die.'"

[4] "You will not surely die," the serpent said to the woman. [5] "For God knows that when you eat of it your eyes will be opened, and you will be like God, knowing good and evil."

[6] When the woman saw that the fruit of the tree was good for food and pleasing to the eye, and also desirable for gaining wisdom, she took some and ate it. She also gave some to her husband, who was with her, and he ate it. [7] Then the eyes of both of them were opened, and they realized they were naked; so they sewed fig leaves together and made coverings for themselves.

[8] Then the man and his wife heard the sound of the Lord God as he was walking in the garden in the cool of the day, and they hid from the Lord God among the trees of the garden. [9] But the Lord God called to the man, "Where are you?"

[10] He answered, "I heard you in the garden, and I was afraid because I was naked; so I hid."

[11] And he said, "Who told you that you were naked? Have you eaten from the tree that I commanded you not to eat from?"

[12] The man said, "The woman you put here with me— she gave me some fruit from the tree, and I ate it."

[13] Then the Lord God said to the woman, "What is this you have done?"

The woman said, "The serpent deceived me, and I ate."

6. Utilizing this Biblical text as your script, choose five people, one to read each character's part: the narrator, God, Adam, Eve and the serpent. Describe God's relationship to Adam and Eve. Note verse 8.

_____

_____

_____

_____

7. Why did Adam and Eve hide?

_____

_____

_____

8. Since God knew where Adam had hidden, why did He ask him where he was?

_____

_____

_____

_____

For a moment, imagine life before the fall: no depression, no low self-worth, no doubts. Notice in this passage how the serpent plants the first seeds of doubt about God with his simple question, "Did God really say...?" That phrase sounds hauntingly familiar in my ears. Every doubt that has ever entered my mind had its beginning back there in the garden. The scheme has never changed. You would think that, by now, I would be conscious of the tricks used to get me off track.

9.  What truth about God's presence stands out in:

    a) Genesis 3:1-13?

    _____

    _____

    _____

    _____

    (b) Jeremiah 23:24? "'Can anyone hide in secret places that I cannot see him?' declares the Lord. 'Do not I fill heaven and earth?' declares the Lord."

    _____

    _____

    _____

Read the following account of Jonah's attempt to hide from God:

## JONAH 1:1–17

<sup>1</sup> The word of the LORD came to Jonah son of Amittai:
<sup>2</sup> "Go to the great city of Nineveh and preach against it, because its wickedness has come up before me."

<sup>3</sup> But Jonah ran away from the LORD and headed for Tarshish. He went down to Joppa, where he found a ship bound for that port. After paying the fare, he went aboard and sailed for Tarshish to flee from the LORD.

<sup>4</sup> Then the LORD sent a great wind on the sea, and such a violent storm arose that the ship threatened to break up. <sup>5</sup> All the sailors were afraid and each cried out to his own god. And they threw the cargo into the sea to lighten the ship.

But Jonah had gone below deck, where he lay down and fell into a deep sleep. <sup>6</sup> The captain went to him and said, "How can you sleep? Get up and call on your god! Maybe he will take notice of us, and we will not perish."

<sup>7</sup> Then the sailors said to each other, "Come, let us cast lots to find out who is responsible for this calamity." They cast lots and the lot fell on Jonah.

<sup>8</sup> So they asked him, "Tell us, who is responsible for making all this trouble for us? What do you do? Where do you come from? What is your country? From what people are you?"

⁹ He answered, "I am a Hebrew and I worship the LORD, the God of heaven, who made the sea and the land."

¹⁰ This terrified them and they asked, "What have you done?" (They knew he was running away from the LORD, because he had already told them so.)

¹¹ The sea was getting rougher and rougher. So they asked him, "What should we do to you to make the sea calm down for us?"

¹² "Pick me up and throw me into the sea," he replied, "and it will become calm. I know that it is my fault that this great storm has come upon you."

¹³ Instead, the men did their best to row back to land. But they could not, for the sea grew even wilder than before. ¹⁴ Then they cried to the LORD, "O LORD, please do not let us die for taking this man's life. Do not hold us accountable for killing an innocent man, for you, O LORD, have done as you pleased." ¹⁵ Then they took Jonah and threw him overboard, and the raging sea grew calm. ¹⁶ At this the men greatly feared the LORD, and they offered a sacrifice to the LORD and made vows to him.

¹⁷ But the LORD provided a great fish to swallow Jonah, and Jonah was inside the fish three days and three nights.

10. What happened when Jonah tried to hide from God?

_____

_____

11. Have you ever tried to hide from God? How? What was the result? Is there any place to escape God? Verify your answer.

_____

_____

_____

Hiding from God is as childish as playing hide-and-seek with little children who are convinced that if their faces are covered, they cannot be seen.

"Any attempt to hide from God does not keep God from seeing me but keeps me from seeing God." *(author unknown)*

12. Read these scriptures and note the significant truths:

(a) "Nothing in all creation is hidden from God's sight. Everything is uncovered and laid bare before the eyes of him to whom we must give account." (Hebrews 4:13 NASB)

_____

_____

_____

(b) "Let your character be free from the love of
money, being content with what you have; for He
Himself has said, 'I will never leave you, nor will I
ever forsake you.'" (Hebrews 13:5 NASB)

_____

_____

_____

Further to the truth that God is everywhere, those who have believed on the name of Jesus have a new place to live.

## ACTS 17:27–28

<sup>27</sup> "God did this so that men would seek him and per-
haps reach out for him and find him, though he is not
far from each one of us. <sup>28</sup> 'For in him we live and move
and have our being.'"

13. Where do we live now that we belong to
Christ?

_____

_____

_____

As we get to know our Heavenly Father more intimately, we can
enjoy His presence on a regular basis, every moment of the day. To embrace this truth daily is a life-changing habit.

14. What does the child's name mean in the following verse? Who is the son?

> "The virgin will be with child and will give birth to a son, and they will call him Immanuel—which means, 'God with us.'" (Matthew 1:23)

_____

_____

_____

_____

It can't be much clearer than that. He is with us, even in us. Rejoice, dance and sing. No longer do I need to listen to the seeds of doubt sprouting, sending choking vines, threatening my very breath. I'll say it again: "He is with me."

15. Where is His dwelling according to this verse?

> "The Word became flesh and made his dwelling among us. We have seen his glory, the glory of the One and Only, who came from the Father, full of grace and truth." (John 1:14)

_____

_____

_____

_____

16. What is the *mystery* according to the following verse? What does that mean to you?

> "To them God has chosen to make known among the Gentiles the glorious riches of this mystery, which is Christ in you, the hope of glory." (Colossians 1:27)

_____

_____

_____

I shout "hallelujah", for I do not have to wait for this wonderful mystery, it is a reality now. If you have repented and confessed Him as Lord, Jesus lives in you. You can't see Him, but He is real and very near.

## JOHN 20:24–31

24 Now Thomas (called Didymus), one of the Twelve, was not with the disciples when Jesus came. 25 So the other disciples told him, "We have seen the Lord!"

But he said to them, "Unless I see the nail marks in his hands and put my finger where the nails were, and put my hand into his side, I will not believe it."

26 A week later his disciples were in the house again, and Thomas was with them. Though the doors were locked, Jesus came and stood among them and said, "Peace be with you!" 27 Then he said to Thomas, "Put your finger here; see my hands. Reach out your hand and put it into my side. Stop doubting and believe."

[28] Thomas said to him, "My Lord and my God!"

[29] Then Jesus told him, "Because you have seen me, you have believed; blessed are those who have not seen and yet have believed."

[30] Jesus did many other miraculous signs in the presence of his disciples, which are not recorded in this book. [31] But these are written that you may believe that Jesus is the Christ, the Son of God, and that by believing you may have life in his name.

17. Note what Thomas exclaims when he realizes that Jesus is with him.

_____

_____

_____

_____

18. What was your response when you realized that Jesus, through the Holy Spirit, lives within you?

_____

_____

_____

_____

19. This week, watch for times when God displays His presence. List several of those majestic moments here. Add to the list throughout this course.

1. _____

2. _____

3. _____

4. _____

5. _____

6. _____

7. _____

8. _____

9. _____

10. _____

11. _____

12. _____

The unchangeable truth, according to God's Word, is that I cannot escape His presence for He is everywhere. What can change, however, is my awareness that He desires to walk beside me, even in me, but awaits my permission to do so. Today you may welcome Him into your life. He only asks that you repent of your sins, then choose to do life His way. The truth is that He is everywhere, not to judge, but to bring life, for He said, "I have come that they may have life, and that they may have it more abundantly." (John 10:10b, NKJV)

His omnipresence assures me that He is closer than the mention of His name. He will lead me. He will guide me. His right hand shall hold me.

## God is everywhere

## God is with me (_____)

Print your name on the line above

## POINTS TO PONDER:

"Where there is devotional music, God is always at hand with his gracious presence."

JOHANN SEBASTIAN BACH

*German composer, musician 1685-1750*

"It boggles my mind that someone can see life breathed into a baby, watch the grass die and then come to life again, see leaves fall and watch the rebirth of a tree, or gaze on any of the majestic splendour that is this earth and not be overpowered by the power of an almighty God."

BILL MCCARTNEY

*American football coach, University of Colorado, President of Promise Keepers*

## TO HIDE IN MY HEART:

"Even there your hand will guide me, your right hand will hold me fast." (Psalm 139:10)

_____

_____

_____

_____

_____

_____

_____

_____

_____

_____

_____

_____

_____

_____

_____

_____

_____

_____

_____

_____

_____

_____

_____

_____

_____

_____

_____

_____

_____

_____

_____

_____

_____

_____

_____

_____

_____

_____

_____

_____

_____

_____

_____

_____

_____

# *Lesson Three*
## GOD CREATED ME

*My antique doll is worth a lot,*

*She brings a memory*

*When I was just a little girl,*

*I threw her in a tree*

*I didn't want to hurt her*

*Just wanted a bit of fun*

*Playing with three sisters*

*Until we were all done*

*I'm glad her value wasn't lost by things that I had done*

*For she was made in Germany in 1901.*

Now that little poem may reveal my lack of poetic ability, but the sentiments are all true. When my mom was in grade school, she had a favourite teacher, Alice Titus. The bond between teacher and student deepened as years went on, and continued until Mrs. Titus died. During her later years, she gave my mother four of her antique dolls, one for each of her daughters. One very memorable day, Mom let me hold the special gift, providing unexpected delight. I took my claimed treasure outside, for I thought that was where all good play took place. She weighed little and I readily threw her in the air. I imagined how she must love the thrill of going up, and the stomach lurch coming down. Of course, at my age, I never managed to break the fall. A doll to play with, that's all that mattered to me. Much to my chagrin, Mom finally put the dolls away. Soon they were all forgotten.

Years rolled by, several moves took place, and eventually I left home to start my independent lifestyle. Teaching, marriage, and two little boys later, I frequently visited my parents' home. One day, Mom looked at me. "If you want one of those antique dolls, you need to get it now, for I'm not moving them again. They are worth a lot, you know."

By this time, my interest in antiquities had waned, and I did not even care if I saw the relics. But I went upstairs to the big old trunk, with the tarnished brass rings and black leather handles. I lifted the heavy lid and heard the groan and squeak of seldom-used hinges. The pungent smell of mothballs took my breath away. While I knew they were probably necessary, I turned my head to get a breath of fresh air. *Why would anyone want these dolls?* I picked up one of them. *Of what use will this be?* Tattered hair, aged, soiled garments, crusty, closing eyelids. But then, her face. I could not turn from her. A closer look revealed perfect porcelain.

Maybe, just maybe, I could take her to a doll restorer, and who knows? Perhaps someday I would find a place to display the old toy. Returning home, I put her aside for a few weeks, but frequently went for a look, each time sensing a growing fondness. Little by little she crept into my heart. One day I reached down to the bottom drawer and lifted her up to eye level. The little doll had a porcelain face with tiny nose, eyes that opened and closed, perfectly sculpted lips and ivory teeth that were set neatly behind a slightly open mouth. I took off her outer dress, then, the shabby cotton undergarment, a pair of corsets, bloomers, socks and shoes. I gasped. Her body, made from stuffed white leather, showed signs of meticulous design. With the help of screws and carefully cut and sewn pieces, even her knees bent. As I turned her over, the words appeared: Germany 1901. Engraved on the porcelain of the upper back, just below her neck, the place of her origin was clearly imprinted, placed there by her German craftsman.

With awakened interest, I went to the phone and called the doll hospital just south of our home town of Newmarket. I couldn't wait to give her the attention she needed; a new wig, new clothes and the love she deserved. Did she have any monetary value? While learning more about dolls created at the beginning of the nineteenth century, I discovered the importance of the engraved imprint. Without it, her worth would be in question.

I imagined her German designer carefully creating his masterpiece, giving particular attention to each detail of her face, hair, torso, arms and legs. And before she left his care, he had made sure that all would know that she had a maker, and he left a stamp to prove it. Her value was not based on what had been done to her, that she had been abused, mistreated and then forgotten. The proof of her worth was engraved on her forever.

1.  What does this scripture say to you about what
    you mean to God? "See, I have engraved you
    on the palms of my hands." (Isaiah 49:16 a)

_____

_____

_____

Often, the things that happen to us in our youth stay with us forever. An unhappy childhood, abuse and rejection fill our minds with a sense of worthlessness. Added to that, in our culture, beauty has become the focal point of significance.

Mary, a participant in one of my Woman of Worth classes, discovered something about her own identity. As she put it, "I never felt thin enough, pretty enough or smart enough. These thoughts hindered me and stopped me from pursuing my dreams."

After my antique doll story, Mary felt compelled to make an engraving on herself to remind her of what her maker had done for her, so that she would never forget her identity in Christ. "I looked up God in Hebrew and found the word for maker," Mary told me. "Then, remembering a poem given to me by my boss, which stated that we never criticize a rosebud for not being a rose, I thought of the thorns on a rose, which made me think of the pain in my life. God uses the pain and the sadness to mould us into what He originally created us to be. I took all those ideas and created a tattoo. I paid the artist to listen to me talk about God as he drew the design on the back of my neck. Now I have a reminder of my identity, of the one who has placed His stamp on me." Mary had finally embraced the truth of her worth, and now has a life-long reminder.

If my doll could talk, what would she say? Would it be, "I don't like my nose. It is so pointy. My legs are too thin (I can't imagine anyone saying that), I'm not worth anything. I'm useless. I've been abused and forgotten. Nobody cares at all for me." And if she did say such things, how would her maker respond?

It is natural for a woman to desire beauty but the huge emphasis on youth and beauty in our culture often causes dissatisfaction with one's own imperfections.

A. Now let's evaluate our own external and internal characteristics. I will explain about the Ns and Ps on the next page, but for now, list six of your external features; height, weight, eye and hair colour, complexion, etc.

( ) 1.                     ( ) 4.

( ) 2.                     ( ) 5.

( ) 3.                     ( ) 6.

Total Ns=___             Total Ps=___

B. List six of your internal characteristics; dreams, secrets, fears, spirituality, moral integrity, creativity, etc.

( ) 1.                     ( ) 4.

( ) 2.                     ( ) 5.

( ) 3.                     ( ) 6.

Total Ns=___             Total Ps=___

Grand total (A&B) of Ns=___     Grand total (A&B) of Ps=___

Inside the brackets, to the left of each numeral, write the letter N if you view the characteristic negatively, or P if you view the characteristic positively. Add up the number of Ps and Ns. Do you have more positives or more negatives? What does this exercise reveal?

_____

_____

_____

One of the goals of this course is to change some of the Ns to Ps.

2.  If you could change one of those negatives, which one would it be? Why?

    _____

    _____

    _____

3.  On what do you base your ideas and thoughts about yourself? Share with the group both the *negative* and *positive* impact that others have had on you. (Include teachers, parents, friends, employees, etc.) Allow 3-5 minutes for each participant so all have an opportunity to share.

    _____

    _____

    _____

It's easy to compare oneself to what appears to be the picture of perfection in magazines, on television, and in the movies. A few years ago, however, while being photographed for Women Alive, I was made acutely aware of the effects of modern technology. By the time the photographer had taken off age spots, raised a drooping eye and touched up the other imperfections, I was concerned I might not be recognized when I arrived at an event. Our self-worth should not be based on appearance. What a relief.

4. Name one experience in your life that has given you a sense of worth.

_____

_____

_____

5. *Guilt* is cited to be the number one destroyer of self worth. What experience has threatened your sense of worth, causing you to doubt your value?

_____

_____

_____

God's values are in total opposition to ours. 1 Samuel 16: 7(b) says, "The Lord does not look at the things that man looks at. Man looks at the outward appearance, but the Lord looks at the heart." Here are some more opposites:

| HUMAN VALUES: | GOD VALUES: |
|---|---|
| Looks | Character |
| Brains | Attitude |
| Wealth | Generosity |
| Talent | Faithfulness |

What makes me a *woman of worth*? Is it what I do, what I own, or who I know? Often, I am so desperate to feel important, that I lose all perspective of the fact that I have a Maker. His imprint on my life gives me value that no one can take away. No circumstance can rob me of my original design.

Some things that I have said do not honour the Master Designer, who had a plan and purpose from before the foundations of the earth. Whether you were conceived in lust or in love, God initiated the fertilized egg, and knit you together in your mother's womb. You are a unique, divine design.

Let's look at the largest organ of our body, the skin. In his book, *Your Skin,* Joseph P. Bark writes, "When you think about this magnificent suit we've been given to 'cover our innards', it renews itself and heals itself so well that it needs no more than minimal cleanliness and repair from time to time. The skin is the most efficient air-conditioning system ever known. Blood flow through the skin is extremely effective in heat transfer to the outside environment from the internal one. If we didn't have many of the components of skin, we would die of cold exposure. The skin's blood vessels clamp shut to preserve our core heat vital to life anytime we are exposed to cold. The skin's fat layer (although many wish they had less fat layer!) acts like a thick layer of insulation for the vital structures below."[8]

---

8  Joseph P. Bark, M.D, *Your Skin* (Englewood Cliffs, NJ: Prentice Hall Press, 1995), 2, 3.

And to think our skin never wears out. "A perfect suit covering the body, fitting every crevice, and as it ages it only sags a little." Well, some of you may think you have a lot of sag but WOW! That is only a little tidbit about a single part of your body. What a creation, each one, a 'one-of a-kind', not to be repeated again.

In her book, *Princess: The True Story of Life Behind the Veil in Saudi Arabia*, Jean Sasson tells of the impact of a woman's life in that country through an interview with Princess, the main character. "The history of our women is buried behind the black veil of secrecy. Neither our births nor our deaths are made official in any public record. Although births of male children are documented in family or tribal records, none are maintained anywhere for females. The common emotion expressed at the birth of a female is either sorrow or shame. I have often asked myself, does this mean we women of the desert do not exist, if our coming and passing goes unrecorded? If no one knows of my existence, does that mean that I do not exist?"[9]

I wish I could share the truths we are studying with Princess.

It is not only in such countries that women feel like that. Right here in North America, there are many women who struggle daily with a lack of purpose and value. Perhaps you are one of those women.

In Lesson One, we established the importance of knowing God in order to rightly evaluate our worth. As we continue our study of Psalm 139, ask God to show you how to apply these truths to your life. *Application* is an important step in Bible study.

---

9   Jean Sasson, *Princess: A True Story of Life Behind the Veil in Saudi Arabia* (Van Nuys, CA: Windsor-Brooke Books, 2001), 23.

## VERSES 13-18

6. What characteristic(s) of God do we find in these verses? Record these below as well as on the lines provided on page 10.

_____

_____

_____

7. Where was God when you were conceived in your mother's womb? What role did God have? Are there any situations that exclude God's control over the creation of a human being? (i.e. rape)

_____

_____

_____

"In a speck of watery material smaller than the dot over this 'i', all the future characteristics of the child are programmed—the colour of his skin, eyes and hair, the shape of his facial features, the natural abilities he will have. All that the child will be physically and mentally is contained in germ form in that fertilized egg." *(Believers Bible Commentary)*[10]

---

10  William MacDonald, *Believer's Bible Commentary* (Nashville, TN: Thomas Nelson Publishers, Inc., 1989), 770.

8. Describe God's divine engineering in verse 13. What does "knit me together" describe? Perhaps some of you enjoy the craft of knitting and will readily see the picture.

_____

_____

_____

"From the fertilized egg will develop: 60 trillion cells, 100 thousand miles of nerve fibre, 60 thousand miles of vessels carrying blood around the body, 250 bones, to say nothing of joints, ligaments and muscles." *(Believers Bible Commentary)*

9. Discuss "made in secret" and "the depths of the earth." (verse 15)

_____

_____

_____

One of God's names is El Roi, "the God who *sees*". We first see this characteristic of God in Genesis 16:13:

"Then she called the name of the LORD who spoke to her, 'You are a God who sees'; for she said, 'Have I even remained alive here after seeing Him?'"

If time permits, read the entire chapter to discover the setting of the *God who sees.*

10. **Verse 16.** Even before the fetus is unwrapped, God sees it and delights in His creation. Write your thoughts here.

_____

_____

_____

Read the following scriptures. Note how far and for whom God is present and creatively active in each passage.

"But when God, who set me apart from birth and called me by his grace, was pleased to reveal his Son in me so that I might preach him among the Gentiles, I did not consult any man." (Galatians 1:15-16a)

_____

_____

_____

"But the Lord said to him, 'Go, for he is a chosen instrument of Mine, to bear My name before the Gentiles and kings and the sons of Israel...'" (Acts 9:15 NASB)

_____

_____

_____

"Before I formed you in the womb I knew you, and be-fore you were born I consecrated you; I have appointed you a prophet to the nations." (Jeremiah 1:5 NASB)

_____

_____

_____

"Listen to Me, O islands, And pay attention, you peoples from afar. The Lord called Me from the womb; From the body of My mother He named Me. (Isaiah 49:1 NASB)

_____

_____

_____

Using a stamp pad, place your fingerprint in the square below. Consider this: yours is a unique, divine design, one of a kind. In light of this, write your thoughts beside the square below.

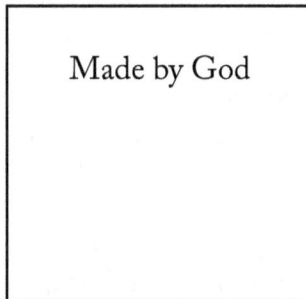

```
┌─────────────────────────┐
│                         │
│      Made by God        │
│                         │
│                         │
│                         │
│                         │
│                         │
└─────────────────────────┘
```

Read Genesis 1:27 NASB: "God created man in His own image, in the image of God He created him; male and female He created them."

11. How were we created?

_____

_____

_____

12. What similarities do we share with our Creator?

_____

_____

_____

13. How can you reflect the image of God?

_____

_____

_____

Dolls made at the turn of the twentieth century served two purposes; one, for a little girl to play with, and two, to provide a visual for fashion design. The ladies of the court assembled in a large room where many dolls had been dressed in the current fashions of the day. The seamstress stitched a dress of the woman's choice from the doll models.

We too are created with and for a purpose. In *Woman of Worship*, we will explore God's plan more fully, but for now let's pray that each of us will come to know our divine purpose—discovering all we need to know to live a rich, full life.

The value God places on each of us is affirmed by Christ's death. Separated from His father, Jesus carried our sins so we could live with Him forever: our worth is wrapped up in His investment in us.

On occasion, I change my doll's elegant wraps to blue jeans and a t-shirt. This outfit reminds me that each of us has designer genes that we wear every day. They show up in our DNA. God has gone to great detail to ensure that we all have our own unique individuality.

14. Have any of your negatives turned to positives after this lesson? Write about that here.

_____

_____

_____

15. How can I reflect the image of God as I think about my own worth?

_____

_____

_____

16. Take time now to write your thoughts about your body. Consider the marvelous creation that you are.

_____

_____

_____

_____

_____

_____

_____

_____

_____

Even in the body of believers, the human tendency is to compare ourselves to others, thinking perhaps that those on the platform are more necessary than those who fold the bulletins. However, 1 Corinthians 12:12-27 reminds us that every part of the body is honourable and important.

## God created everyone

## God created me (_____)

Print your name on the line above

## Points to ponder:

"Techniques for improving one's self-esteem include identifying, understanding and celebrating your uniqueness. Since we all have strengths and weaknesses, focus on your strengths—the God given gifts that are needed for encouraging and serving others."

Dr. Libby Skidmore

"The imprint of the Father remains forever on the life of the child."

Roy Lessin

## To hide in my heart:

"I praise you because I am fearfully and wonderfully made; your works are wonderful, I know that full well." (Psalm 139: 14)

_____

_____

_____

_____

_____

_____

---

---

---

---

---

---

---

---

---

---

---

---

---

_____

_____

_____

_____

_____

_____

_____

_____

_____

_____

_____

_____

# *Lesson Four*
## GOD DEFENDS ME

The phone rang, piercing the stillness of the late hour. Keith's* voice quivered, then broke. "Marilyn* has left and taken Stephen*. I don't know where she is and I don't think she is coming back." The words drove into me like the thrust of a knife. My heart stopped beating as our son uttered his devastating news. A flashback to earlier days brought memories of his first year in university. I instantly recalled the night Keith had invited Bob and me to his apartment to tell us that his girlfriend carried his baby, our first grandchild.

Overwhelming thoughts crowded every crevice of my mind as I pondered their individual athletic achievements, and their dreams for the future. Picking up the pieces, they decided to create their own home, and later that fall made their vows before a small family gathering. In

---

* names changed

spite of their challenging beginning, I confidently believed that if we prayed long enough and hard enough, together they would make it. But now, the unravelling had begun.

A couple of weeks later, I invited Marilyn to our home to affirm our love and commitment to her and Keith. I sat on the sofa in our living room and pleaded. "Bob and I will help you in any way we can, get you counselling or whatever you need. I don't want this marriage to end. Is Keith not treating you well?" I questioned my daughter-in-law.

"Oh, Keith is a great guy, a good dad, but we fight a lot."

"Often in marriages our differences need time to be worked out," I offered.

The conversation continued, each of us giving our thoughts. After a few minutes I heard the unwelcome words, "I just don't want to be married anymore."

I felt tears spill out and trickle down my cheeks. *How could this be?* We went to church, tithed, served in the community and trusted God to keep our children from all harm and danger. It just wasn't fair.

Despite Keith's determination to win her back, their covenant, established in a garden wedding just two years earlier, soon ended. Stephen was eighteen months old, an adorable, dark-haired, happy little toddler.

With the stress of university, physical training in his wrestling sport and mental anguish over his failed marriage, Keith's health deteriorated. Seizures plagued him and life became unbearable. He had lost everything he had lived for; his sport, his wife and his little boy. He knew he couldn't go on, so he headed to the river to end his misery. God, in his mercy, placed a mental image of Stephen in his mind and that picture of his little boy, needing him, spared his life.

I prayed desperately every day, pleading with God for something good to come from the devastation, the ripping apart of this union. I naively believed that I could play a part in the restoration. My head spun as I tried to think of ways to help our son's marriage. No parents want to see their child in such despair.

During the next year, more attempts were made to repair the matrimonial damage, but none were successful.

1. What circumstances in your life leave you with the thought, *It's just not fair?* Describe the emotions that surface as you bring these to mind.

_____

_____

_____

All too soon, the divorce papers arrived at his home. D-day but no victory, only destruction. Then the custody battle over their baby began. A court system, that knew nothing about us, had the power to determine the destiny of our first grandchild. Not fair. Stephen, not yet two years old, had done nothing to deserve losing the security of a loving home, and the benefits of a dad and mom being together. He had no control over the decisions of his parents.

Mentally fatigued from all the confusion, I sought advice from a counsellor. It took time to sort out what helped and what hindered in the grief process that inevitably accompanies divorce. I desperately wanted to make things right, but it was not my responsibility. It is God's job to deal with injustice. This week we will explore the last six verses of Psalm 139. Let's stand and read this text, as recorded on page 11.

## PSALM 139: 19-24

2. What characteristics of God do you see in the last six verses? Record these below as well as on the lines provided on page 11.

_____

_____

3. Can you sense David's frustration with *wickedness*? Do you relate to his frustration? If so, how?

_____

_____

4. What does David desire for the *wicked*? Describe the wicked men of bloodshed.

_____

_____

5. Was David's hatred justified? Why or why not?

_____

_____

6. Why are the *wicked* David's enemies?

_____

_____

7.  What injustices have you or your family experienced? How can we hate and yet love?

_____

_____

_____

8.  Why did David ask God to search his heart? The Psalm begins and ends with searching. How does the meaning of the word 'search' change between verse 1 and 23? Can you see a progression in the way David views God as he makes his way through God's characteristics?

_____

_____

_____

As God searches my heart, there are so many things that He could find there, things I hold in my heart against Him or others. I can be bitter, angry, self-righteous, and many more ugly emotions. I can dislike my body, His creation. I can deny God's presence and His power to make all things right.

Throughout the first eighteen verses of Psalm 139, David praised Almighty God for His different characteristics, as we have studied. But in these last verses, he makes some requests.

9.  What does David ask God to do?

_____

_____

_____

10. What could he have been thinking when he asked God to search him so thoroughly? Could it be that David knew from his own experiences just how subtle sin is, so pervasive that it can inhabit every word, thought and deed?

_____

_____

_____

We all need divine help to see ourselves as we really are. In Lesson One, I mentioned how I disliked anyone knowing what went on in my head. During this time of adjustment to our broken family, my thoughts needed searching over and over. I experienced great difficulty separating the wrong done from the person doing it. How could I think such horrible thoughts? I wanted revenge for the pain caused to each member of my family.

11. Are you willing to have your heart searched?

_____

_____

Each time Keith went to court to determine who would have custody, we prayed for God's intervention. The day came for the final decision from the judge. While waiting at home for the verdict, my emotions sank. Sobs came easily as I feared for all three, although, I must be honest, mostly for Keith and Stephen. *Forgive me, Lord.*

Finally the phone rang.

"How did it go?" I bravely asked.

"Not very well, Mom. I get visitation rights only, and just every other weekend." Not enough time for a dad who wants to be with his son daily, wrestling on the floor before supper and tossing a ball with him as he grows up.

*How will Keith ever get through this? What can I say to help him see God in a new way?* I had no answers.

Before I could collect my wandering thoughts and attempt to encourage our son, he spoke, a little whisper of hope in each word. "Mom, during my quiet time this morning, before I left to go to the courthouse, I sensed God saying, "You may not have your son here on earth, but you will have him for all of eternity.""

Not for a moment did I think he would give up on his pursuit to have his son, but Keith's words gave me a little glimpse of God's perspective. Our caring Heavenly Father planted in Keith's heart the assurance that He cared about the pain, the loss, and the wrongs. In the end, God Himself would look after our son's little boy.

David asks God to search him now at the end of the Psalm. Perhaps when we look at evil, we need to do the same. The presence of injustice always provides an opportunity to bring out the worst in all of us.

Let's look at two Biblical examples (one Old and one New Testament) to explore some thoughts about those that have suffered injustices. Why not stand, and take turns reading Joseph's story.

## GENESIS 37:1–34

<sup>1</sup> Jacob lived in the land where his father had stayed, the land of Canaan.

<sup>2</sup> This is the account of Jacob. Joseph, a young man of seventeen, was tending the flocks with his brothers, the sons of Bilhah and the sons of Zilpah, his father's wives, and he brought their father a bad report about them.

<sup>3</sup> Now Israel loved Joseph more than any of his other sons, because he had been born to him in his old age; and he made a richly ornamented robe for him. <sup>4</sup> When his brothers saw that their father loved him more than any of them, they hated him and could not speak a kind word to him.

<sup>5</sup> Joseph had a dream, and when he told it to his brothers, they hated him all the more. <sup>6</sup> He said to them, "Listen to this dream I had: <sup>7</sup> We were binding sheaves of grain out in the field when suddenly my sheaf rose and stood upright, while your sheaves gathered around mine and bowed down to it."

<sup>8</sup> His brothers said to him, "Do you intend to reign over us? Will you actually rule us?" And they hated him all the more because of his dream and what he had said.

<sup>9</sup> Then he had another dream, and he told it to his brothers. "Listen," he said, "I had another dream, and this time the sun and moon and eleven stars were bowing down to me."

<sup>10</sup> When he told his father as well as his brothers, his father rebuked him and said, "What is this dream you

had? Will your mother and I and your brothers actually come and bow down to the ground before you?" [11] His brothers were jealous of him, but his father kept the matter in mind.

[12] Now his brothers had gone to graze their father's flocks near Shechem, [13] and Israel said to Joseph, "As you know, your brothers are grazing the flocks near Shechem. Come, I am going to send you to them."

"Very well," he replied.

[14] So he said to Joseph, "Go and see if all is well with your brothers and with the flocks, and bring word back to me." Then he sent him off from the Valley of Hebron.

When Joseph arrived at Shechem, [15] a man found him wandering around in the fields and asked him, "What are you looking for?"

[16] He replied, "I'm looking for my brothers. Can you tell me where they are grazing their flocks?"

[17] "They have moved on from here," the man answered. "I heard them say, 'Let's go to Dothan.'"

So Joseph went after his brothers and found them near Dothan. [18] But they saw him in the distance, and before he reached them, they plotted to kill him.

[19] "Here comes that dreamer!" they said to each other. [20] "Come now, let's kill him and throw him into one of these cisterns and say that a ferocious animal devoured him. Then we'll see what comes of his dreams."

21 When Reuben heard this, he tried to rescue him from their hands. "Let's not take his life," he said. 22 "Don't shed any blood. Throw him into this cistern here in the desert, but don't lay a hand on him." Reuben said this to rescue him from them and take him back to his father.

23 So when Joseph came to his brothers, they stripped him of his robe—the richly ornamented robe he was wearing— 24 and they took him and threw him into the cistern. Now the cistern was empty; there was no water in it.

25 As they sat down to eat their meal, they looked up and saw a caravan of Ishmaelites coming from Gilead. Their camels were loaded with spices, balm and myrrh, and they were on their way to take them down to Egypt.

26 Judah said to his brothers, "What will we gain if we kill our brother and cover up his blood? 27 Come, let's sell him to the Ishmaelites and not lay our hands on him; after all, he is our brother, our own flesh and blood." His brothers agreed.

28 So when the Midianite merchants came by, his brothers pulled Joseph up out of the cistern and sold him for twenty shekels of silver to the Ishmaelites, who took him to Egypt.

29 When Reuben returned to the cistern and saw that Joseph was not there, he tore his clothes. 30 He went back to his brothers and said, "The boy isn't there! Where can I turn now?"

<sup>31</sup> Then they got Joseph's robe, slaughtered a goat and dipped the robe in the blood. <sup>32</sup> They took the ornamented robe back to their father and said, "We found this. Examine it to see whether it is your son's robe."

<sup>33</sup> He recognized it and said, "It is my son's robe! Some ferocious animal has devoured him. Joseph has surely been torn to pieces."

<sup>34</sup> Then Jacob tore his clothes, put on sackcloth and mourned for his son many days.

12. Who was Joseph? Why did his father, Jacob, show favour to him?

_____

_____

_____

13. What did Jacob do to cause enmity between Joseph and his brothers?

_____

_____

_____

14. What did the brothers decide to do to Joseph?

_____

_____

15. What change in plans took place when the Egyptian caravan came by? Which brother did not like the plan?

_____

_____

_____

16. How much did the Egyptians pay for Joseph? What did that amount of money suggest?

_____

_____

_____

17. How old was Joseph when he was taken from his home and thrust into another environment? List some of the emotions Joseph may have felt as a teenager.

_____

_____

_____

18. Who might he have blamed for this crisis?

_____

_____

Let's read on to find out more about Joseph's unfair circumstances.

## GENESIS 39:1–21

¹ Now Joseph had been taken down to Egypt. Potiphar, an Egyptian who was one of Pharaoh's officials, the captain of the guard, bought him from the Ishmaelites who had taken him there.

² The LORD was with Joseph and he prospered, and he lived in the house of his Egyptian master. ³ When his master saw that the LORD was with him and that the LORD gave him success in everything he did, ⁴ Joseph found favor in his eyes and became his attendant. Potiphar put him in charge of his household, and he entrusted to his care everything he owned. ⁵ From the time he put him in charge of his household and of all that he owned, the LORD blessed the household of the Egyptian because of Joseph. The blessing of the LORD was on everything Potiphar had, both in the house and in the field. ⁶ So he left in Joseph's care everything he had; with Joseph in charge, he did not concern himself with anything except the food he ate.

Now Joseph was well-built and handsome, ⁷ and after a while his master's wife took notice of Joseph and said, "Come to bed with me!"

⁸ But he refused. "With me in charge," he told her, "my master does not concern himself with anything in the house; everything he owns he has entrusted to my care. ⁹ No one is greater in this house than I am. My master has withheld nothing from me except you, because you are

his wife. How then could I do such a wicked thing and sin against God?" [10] And though she spoke to Joseph day after day, he refused to go to bed with her or even be with her.

[11] One day he went into the house to attend to his duties, and none of the household servants was inside. [12] She caught him by his cloak and said, "Come to bed with me!" But he left his cloak in her hand and ran out of the house.

[13] When she saw that he had left his cloak in her hand and had run out of the house, [14] she called her household servants. "Look," she said to them, "this Hebrew has been brought to us to make sport of us! He came in here to sleep with me, but I screamed. [15] When he heard me scream for help, he left his cloak beside me and ran out of the house."

[16] She kept his cloak beside her until his master came home. [17] Then she told him this story: "That Hebrew slave you brought us came to me to make sport of me. [18] But as soon as I screamed for help, he left his cloak beside me and ran out of the house."

[19] When his master heard the story his wife told him, saying, "This is how your slave treated me," he burned with anger. [20] Joseph's master took him and put him in prison, the place where the king's prisoners were confined.

But while Joseph was there in the prison, [21] the LORD was with him; he showed him kindness and granted him favor in the eyes of the prison warden.

19. Why did Joseph experience success in Egypt? Note the verses.

_____

_____

_____

_____

_____

20. Describe his relationship to Potiphar's wife. What kind of character did Joseph have? How did he show his integrity?

_____

_____

_____

_____

21. What story did Potiphar's wife tell her husband? How did he respond?

_____

_____

_____

_____

22. List below some of Joseph's potential thoughts while in prison, falsely accused again.

_____

_____

_____

When time permits, read the continuing saga recorded in chapters 40 to 45. There you will discover more unjust situations that occur in Joseph's life. Genesis 42 begins to unfold the drama of the reuniting of Joseph with his brothers.

23. Read the following passage. How did Joseph evaluate the whole process from the time he was thrown into the pit to the reuniting of his family in Egypt?

GENESIS 45:5–9

[5] "And now, do not be distressed and do not be angry with yourselves for selling me here, because it was to save lives that God sent me ahead of you. [6] For two years now there has been famine in the land, and for the next five years there will not be plowing and reaping. [7] But God sent me ahead of you to preserve for you a remnant on earth and to save your lives by a great deliverance. [8] So then, it was not you who sent me here, but God. He made me father to Pharaoh, lord of his entire household and ruler of all Egypt. [9] Now hurry back to my father and say to him, 'This is what your son Joseph says: God has made me lord of all Egypt. Come down to me; don't delay.'"

_____

_____

_____

24. The following scripture further illustrates Joseph's perspective on the events in his life. Write out his view of the injustices shown him by his brothers.

## GENESIS 50:19-20

[19] But Joseph said to them, "Don't be afraid. Am I in the place of God? [20] You intended to harm me, but God intended it for good to accomplish what is now being done, the saving of many lives."

_____

_____

_____

25. Did Joseph have reason to be bitter? Was he? Explain.

_____

_____

_____

_____

26. Does the exploration of Joseph's story shed any light or any hope on your own situation?

_____

_____

_____

27. What good came from "the pit"?

_____

_____

_____

28. If God is good, why does He allow such unfair experiences to happen to us?

_____

_____

_____

Now we will look at Stephen, a New Testament example:

## ACTS 6:8–15

⁸ Now Stephen, a man full of God's grace and power, did great wonders and miraculous signs among the people. ⁹ Opposition arose, however, from members of the Synagogue of the Freedmen (as it was called)— Jews of Cyrene and Alexandria as well as the provinces

of Cilicia and Asia. These men began to argue with Stephen, <sup>10</sup>but they could not stand up against his wisdom or the Spirit by whom he spoke.

<sup>11</sup> Then they secretly persuaded some men to say, "We have heard Stephen speak words of blasphemy against Moses and against God."

<sup>12</sup> So they stirred up the people and the elders and the teachers of the law. They seized Stephen and brought him before the Sanhedrin. <sup>13</sup> They produced false witnesses, who testified, "This fellow never stops speaking against this holy place and against the law. <sup>14</sup> For we have heard him say that this Jesus of Nazareth will destroy this place and change the customs Moses handed down to us."

<sup>15</sup> All who were sitting in the Sanhedrin looked intently at Stephen, and they saw that his face was like the face of an angel.

29. Of what was Stephen accused? Was he guilty?

_____

_____

30. Describe his countenance during the false accusations. See verse 15.

_____

_____

_____

You can read about Stephen's speech in Acts 7. His words were unpopular and led to his stoning. The following verses record the crowds' reaction to his talk:

## ACTS 7:54–60

[54] When they heard this, they were furious and gnashed their teeth at him. [55] But Stephen, full of the Holy Spirit, looked up to heaven and saw the glory of God, and Jesus standing at the right hand of God. [56] "Look," he said, "I see heaven open and the Son of Man standing at the right hand of God."

[57] At this they covered their ears and, yelling at the top of their voices, they all rushed at him, [58] dragged him out of the city and began to stone him. Meanwhile, the witnesses laid their clothes at the feet of a young man named Saul.

[59] While they were stoning him, Stephen prayed, "Lord Jesus, receive my spirit." [60] Then he fell on his knees and cried out, "Lord, do not hold this sin against them." When he had said this, he fell asleep.

31. What did Stephen see, according to verse 55?

_____

_____

_____

32. Where was Jesus?

_____

_____

Read Hebrews 1:3 and Hebrews 10:12.

³ The Son is the radiance of God's glory and the exact representation of his being, sustaining all things by his powerful word. After he had provided purification for sins, he sat down at the right hand of the Majesty in heaven.

¹² But when this priest had offered for all time one sacrifice for sins, he sat down at the right hand of God.

33. Where is Jesus in these verses?

_____

_____

_____

The above verses indicate that Jesus sat down at the right hand of God, for His work was done. Stephen, though, in Acts 7 on page 90, sees Jesus standing. Could it be that Jesus stood to defend Stephen as a defence lawyer stands to defend his client? Yes. Although His work is done for our salvation, completed through the shedding of His blood on the cross, He still stands to defend us. Can you grasp this truth? It is life-changing, when embraced.

34. Write Stephen's prayer as he died.

_____

_____

_____

The Lord's Prayer is found in Matthew 6:9-13. Verse 12 states, "Forgive us our debts, as we also have forgiven our debtors." Forgiveness does not mean condoning the offence. It only means that you let go of the load of anger, anxiety, and turmoil that rips, tears and causes bitterness. Forgiveness frees us to be all that God intends us to be.

## God defends what is right
## God defends me (_____)

Print your name on the line above

Write here your thoughts on the idea of God being your defender. Use some scripture from this lesson in your answer.

_____

_____

_____

_____

_____

## Points to ponder:

"God's silence is in no way indicative of His inactivity or involvement in our lives. He may be silent but He is not still."

Dr. Charles Stanley

"One who is protected by the merciful Lord—no one can rival him."

Sri Guru Granth Sahib

## To hide in my heart:

"Search me, O God and know my heart; test me and know my anxious thoughts. See if there is any offensive way in me, and lead me in the way everlasting." (Psalm 139:23, 24)

_____

_____

_____

_____

_____

_____

_____

## THROUGH A GLASS DARKLY

*Conflict – for the joy of the fight.*

*They're wrong!*

*It's just that simple.*

*Why won't they see the truth?*

*No prejudice here.*

*I know what I know.*

*Don't confuse me with irrelevant facts.*

*They are so narrow minded.*

*They are so closed to the truth.*

*They...*

*They...*

*That mirror...?*

*That reflection of... They?*

*That face... so familiar*

*But  Still Wrong!*

Copyright Brian Austin, 2005. Used by permission.

_____

_____

_____

_____

_____

_____

_____

_____

_____

_____

_____

_____

_____

_____

_____

_____

_____

_____

_____

_____

_____

_____

_____

_____

_____

_____

_____

_____

_____

_____

_____

_____

_____

_____

_____

_____

_____

_____

_____

# CONCLUSION

Wow! You have finished Book 1 of the expanded *WOW* series, *Woman of Worth*.

What is the most significant truth that you have gleaned from this study? How will you apply this truth to your life?

_____

_____

_____

_____

_____

My prayer is that you will live each day in light of God's characteristics. No matter how you think or feel, or if it seems otherwise some days, you are loved unconditionally. Let God's Word be the indicator of truth. He created you. He knows you. He is with you. He defends and protects you. Now that is a Father worth loving and serving.

My friend, I am so happy that you joined me on this journey of understanding your worth in God's eyes. Consider standing as a group and saying together, "I am a woman of worth…WOW!" Delight your Creator by repeating this phrase often. He has never made anyone without value and purpose. That is who He is.

I would love to hear how God has used this study to strengthen your faith. Email me ruth@wordstoinspire.ca.

Don't miss the next book in this series, *Woman of the Word*, which explores practical ways to incorporate scripture into your life. This will help you to resist temptation and will also encourage you in your journey. Included is a step-by-step process for your group to memorize Psalm 8 together. *Woman of the Word* can also be done as an individual study.

# Bibliography

## Lesson One:

Blackaby, Henry T. and Claude V. King. *Experiencing God*. Nashville, TN: Broadman & Holman Publishers, 1994.

MacDonald, William. *Believer's Bible Commentary*. Nashville, TN: Thomas Nelson Publishers, Inc., 1989.

Mullen, Grant. *Why Do I Feel So Down When My Faith Should Lift Me Up?* Kent, England: Sovereign World, 1999.

Strong, James, S.T.D., LL.D. *Strong's Exhaustive Concordance of the Bible*. Iowa Falls, IA: Riverside Book and Bible House.

## Lesson Two:

Lucado, Max. *The Applause of Heaven*. Dallas, TX: Word Publishing, 1990.

Moore, Beth. *Believing God*. Nashville, TN: Broadman & Holman Publishing Group, 2004.

## Lesson Three:

Bark, Joseph P., M.D. *Your Skin*. Englewood Cliffs, NJ: Prentice Hall Press, 1995.

MacDonald, William. *Believer's Bible Commentary*. Nashville, TN: Thomas Nelson Publishers, Inc., 1989.

Sasson, Jean. *Princess: A True Story of Life Behind the Veil in Saudi Arabia*. Van Nuys, CA: Windsor-Brooke Books, 2001.


LESSON FOUR:

Austin, Brian. "Through A Glass Darkly." Durham, ON, 2005. Used by permission.

Strong, James, S.T.D., LL.D. *Strong's Exhaustive Concordance of the Bible*. Iowa Falls, IA: Riverside Book and Bible House.

Learn More About *Words To Inspire* and the *WOW* Series

For more information and to purchase product go to:
www.wordstoinspire.ca
FB Ruth Coghill

To contact Ruth:
ruth@wordstoinspire.ca
ruthcoghill@gmail.com

www.ingramcontent.com/pod-product-compliance
Lightning Source LLC
Chambersburg PA
CBHW060156070426
42447CB00033B/1881